Who is
The Christ?

CWR

Anne Calver

© CWR 2018

Published 2018 by CWR, Waverley Abbey House, Waverley Lane, Farnham, Surrey GU9 8EP, UK. CWR is a Registered Charity – Number 294387 and a Limited Company registered in England – Registration Number 1990308.

The right of Anne Calver to her own writings has been asserted by her in accordance with the Copyright, Designs and Patents Act 1988, sections 77 and 78.

For a list of National Distributors, visit cwr.org.uk/distributors

Scripture references are taken from The Holy Bible, New International Version® Anglicised, NIV® Copyright © 1979, 1984, 2011 by Biblica, Inc.® Used by permission. All rights reserved worldwide.

Concept development, editing, design and production by CWR.

Every effort has been made to ensure that this book contains the correct permissions and references, but if anything has been inadvertently overlooked the Publisher will be pleased to make the necessary arrangements at the first opportunity. Please contact the Publisher directly.

Cover image: Adobestock

Printed in the UK by Linney

ISBN: 978-1-78259-760-5

Contents

Introduction

Lent is a time for us to make space to meet with the Lord. Whether or not we choose to fast from some meals or give up something that is taking up too much room in our lives, this is an exciting season of seeking the face of God through His Word and by the power of His Spirit.

Lent leads us towards Easter: it is the journey to Calvary, to the cross and ultimately to the resurrection of our Saviour three days later. As we journey together throughout the next 40 days, let's reflect on Jesus' path to His own death, and ask Him to speak to us about how He wants us to walk with Him. What does it really look like to deny ourselves, take up our cross daily and follow Him (Luke 9:23)?

Many years ago, I had a dream about being part of a group walking to Calvary. We had decided that we wanted to walk the walk that Jesus had done to the cross. It was hot, and the sun was beating down on us. We wore simple clothes and sandals on our feet. Our provisions quickly ran out, and we soon felt exhausted and thirsty. One by one, grumbling voices began: 'I'm thirsty'; 'My feet hurt'; 'I can't do this...' Eventually the voices grew louder, and I found myself thinking that I too had had enough. I looked down at my feet – they were bleeding from rubbing on rocks. I looked up at my companions and they were sunburnt and dehydrated. We walked slower and slower until we finally decided to stop and to call for the bus to come and meet us on the road. We could go no further.

I climbed onto the bus with the others and collapsed in a crumpled heap, calling for water and hanging my head. Then I heard the voice of God: *What do you think you are doing, Anne?* Immediately, I responded: 'I can't do it, Lord. It's too hard. I don't know how You did it – I'm too tired and weak.' I made my complaints and I waited: no response. I knew deep in my gut that I had to get off the bus.

I slowly and reluctantly stood to my feet and said, 'I'm going to keep walking, is anyone coming with me?' My husband stood, as did a few others (but not the people I would have expected –

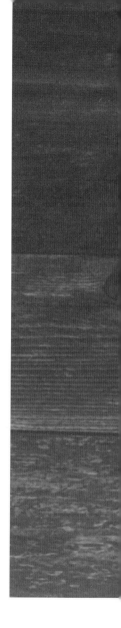

not the strong, popular or capable), and we got off the bus. My dream continued as we walked up towards where Jesus died for us. The pain did not leave my body, nor did my thirst disappear – but the joy in my heart outweighed the physical struggle. I knew I was going where God wanted me to. I heard these words just before I woke up: 'whoever wants to save their life will lose it, but whoever loses their life for me will find it' (Matt. 16:25).

The subjects in this study are all about our journey to Calvary, and ultimately to a resurrected life. We cannot 'take up our cross' without allowing Jesus' story to change our story by the power of the Holy Spirit, until we finally become like Him. Therefore the titles of each session reflect some aspects of the nature and character of our God, leading us to really dwell on who He is and the marks that He left on the world. As we make our way through these studies of who Jesus is, allow His story to speak to yours: how does who He is change who you want to be? Let's ask ourselves: what was Jesus seeking to build and is what we are building similar? More importantly, are we building a life that is rooted and grounded in Christ? Are we pleasing ourselves or our King? Our God is a holy God, and Jesus was tempted but without sin; do we need to refocus on the holiness of the three in one, asking what difference that makes to our lives?

I'd also like us to spend some time reflecting on the fact that God is in the business of harvesting – growing us up as strong witnesses in a world of weeds and hostility. Jesus had to navigate His way through the world and overcome the tactics of the enemy, so what can we learn from Him about standing firm until Christ brings in the harvest? How do we move from death to life? And finally, in response to Jesus' call to 'feed His lambs', are we just self-seeking, or surrendering and serving our Lord with all that He has given to us?

The way of the cross is not an easy road, but it is the most life-giving journey we can ever be on. Our Lord longs for us to journey closely with Him every day – not holding tightly to the way of the world but following the way of His Spirit. Life in all its fullness is not just reserved for eternity – our King wants us to access it now by building in His name, serving one

another, laying down our own agenda, seeking holiness and purity, standing strong in relationship with Him, being free and knowing we are sent. However, the most important thing about Lent – or any day for that matter – is holding on to the reality that Jesus loves us more than anything in the world, and that is why He went to the cross for you and for me.

The Builder

'Unless the LORD builds the house, the builders labour in vain.' (Psa. 127:1)

Icebreaker

Ask each person to think of their favourite famous building in the world and then describe it to the members in the group. Everyone else tries to guess which building it is. Explain to each other why that particular building is your favourite. (Alternatively, play a game of Jenga!)

Opening Prayer

Thank You, Lord Jesus, that You are the chief builder, the cornerstone of our lives and our Church. We praise You for everything that You have built and continue to build in our lives and communities. Please help us to seek first Your kingdom and Your righteousness, and to discover more of what it means to build our lives in You. Amen.

Eye Opener

Demolishing a building takes a lot of work. An undermining process is often instigated, which mainly happens at the base of the building and controls the manner and direction in which it will fall. Other demolition tactics include the weakening of support columns, a controlled explosion, or a good old-fashioned wrecking ball! In the game Jenga, individual blocks of a precariously balanced structure are removed until, eventually, just one removed piece will be what causes the whole tower to topple over.

The foundation that we build on, and the materials used to build, affect how quickly our structures come down or how long they will last.

Setting the Scene

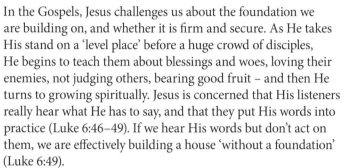

In the Gospels, Jesus challenges us about the foundation we are building on, and whether it is firm and secure. As He takes His stand on a 'level place' before a huge crowd of disciples, He begins to teach them about blessings and woes, loving their enemies, not judging others, bearing good fruit – and then He turns to growing spiritually. Jesus is concerned that His listeners really hear what He has to say, and that they put His words into practice (Luke 6:46–49). If we hear His words but don't act on them, we are effectively building a house 'without a foundation' (Luke 6:49).

In Matthew 7:24–27, Jesus is talking to His followers about building their faith. Before He tells the parable of the wise and foolish builders, He again teaches first about the fruit we bear, and the importance of not judging others. Jesus is also keen to emphasise the importance of asking, seeking and knocking, as well as the need to identify the narrow road we are to walk down with Him. Perhaps Jesus addresses all these things to outline how we can build on a firm foundation. You can imagine Him becoming quite passionate as He speaks the words in this passage, conveying the urgency of His message – it's important that we get this into our heads!

Bible Readings

Luke 6:46–49
'Why do you call me, "Lord, Lord," and do not do what I say? As for everyone who comes to me and hears my words and puts them into practice, I will show you what they are like. They are like a man building a house, who dug down deep and laid the foundation on rock. When the flood came, the torrent struck that house but could not shake it, because it was well built. But the one who hears my words and does not put them into practice is like a man who built a house on the ground without a foundation. The moment the torrent struck that house, it collapsed and its destruction was complete.'

Matthew 7:24–27

'Therefore everyone who hears these words of mine and puts them into practice is like a wise man who built his house on the rock. The rain came down, the streams rose, and the winds blew and beat against that house; yet it did not fall, because it had its foundation on the rock. But everyone who hears these words of mine and does not put them into practice is like a foolish man who built his house on sand. The rain came down, the streams rose, and the winds blew against that house, and it fell with a great crash.'

Session Focus

Just down the road from where we live in North London, there is a big primary school that recently had to close its doors. It was very sudden – in only a matter of hours, the children were told that they could not attend the school for the foreseeable future, and the teachers were suddenly out of a job. Needless to say, the local community has been in uproar! It turns out that the school was built on an old chalk mine back in the 1800s, and slowly but surely, the building had been sinking into what was basically a giant sink-hole. The school had been built on a very uncertain foundation and was becoming extremely dangerous to be in. From the outside, everything looked normal – a great big brick building, a school that was flourishing – yet it closed overnight. As I write, the pupils are having to commute 15 minutes by bus to a couple of different schools (much to the frustration of local residents).

In the Bible passages we've just read, Jesus is reiterating to His followers that the only sure foundation is Him: building *in* Him and building on His words. Christ is the chief cornerstone of our faith, the only one who will enable us to build something sustainable. If we choose to build on sand (a substance similar to chalk, which can move and sink), we take our eyes off the key builder, choosing the world's way – which is not at all solid, reliable or dependable. Jesus doesn't mention sand in Luke's Gospel, but He talks about a building with no foundation.

Only digging deep into the truth of Christ's words will help us to build a firm foundation that will not give way.

In the story of the three little pigs, the house of sticks has no chance when the wolf huffs and puffs and blows it down! But the wise little pig in the house of bricks is safe. It may take time to build something strong and in the right way, but Jesus is saying, 'Keep going, it is worth it!' In our instant western culture, it can be hard to think more long-term; we get bored easily, feel impatient when change doesn't happen, and we want things *now*! I can easily imagine being like the little pig who built his house with sticks, because it would have been so much quicker and simpler than brick. But, of course, it wouldn't last long.

Nehemiah spent time and energy rebuilding the walls of Jerusalem with a team of builders and watchmen. He covered his back, and considered the whole picture. Jesus is calling His followers to commit to build with Him and others, not to be side-tracked by short-term fixes. The call on our lives to build well is increasingly challenged by our 'fix it quick or bin it now' world, but we can start by building holy habits into our daily lives. To keep discovering more of Christ, let's not give up reading the Bible or praying or sharing fellowship with believers, and witnessing to a broken world. These disciplines, empowered by the Holy Spirit, lead us into vibrant life in Christ and are part of building a firm foundation.

My brother-in-law used to own a t-shirt that read: 'He who dies with the most toys, still dies.' This can give us such a helpful perspective when we find ourselves falling into the trap of materialism or comparing ourselves with others. We can build our lives on the things of this world, but they will not last forever. Sand shifts and changes – it cannot be trusted and will eventually cave in or disappear. None of the pupils or teachers in our local school would have imagined that their lives would change so much in a matter of days. We can feel secure in buildings and relationships, but the only one who can sustain and satisfy us completely is Jesus. We will face storms in this life. There are wolves in sheep's clothing. Jesus is clear that life is not an easy road, and that is why He addresses our foundations. In the busy lead up to Easter, when challenges come, the call of Christ is to keep building in Him, seeking His face.

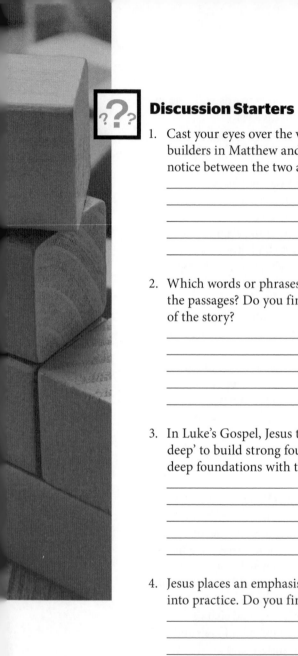

Discussion Starters

1. Cast your eyes over the verses of the wise and foolish builders in Matthew and Luke. What differences do you notice between the two accounts?

2. Which words or phrases particularly speak to you from the passages? Do you find those words in both accounts of the story?

3. In Luke's Gospel, Jesus talks about a man who 'dug down deep' to build strong foundations. Have you had to dig deep foundations with the Lord? How have you done that?

4. Jesus places an emphasis on hearing and putting His words into practice. Do you find it easy to do that?

5. Have you ever faced storms in your life that have made you question the strength of your foundations?

_____

_____

_____

_____

_____

6. Have you ever felt like the foolish man building on sand? In what ways? Did you try to change what you were doing?

_____

_____

_____

_____

_____

7. What storms are most likely to cause your 'house' to come down?

_____

_____

_____

_____

_____

8. What can you change in your life to build your life in Christ?

_____

_____

_____

_____

_____

Final Thoughts

Back in the 1990s, there was a deadly hurricane in Tegucigalpa, Honduras. Entire villages were wiped out, and there were over 19,000 casualties recorded as a result. This was Hurricane Mitch, the second deadliest Atlantic hurricane on record. Huge mudslides swept down the hills, suffocating homes and people. My father-in-law was working for World Relief at the time, and was able to go into Tegucigalpa to raise awareness and generate support for those remaining. He tells the story of walking through the streets and seeing houses buried under a blanket of mud, one with a single crutch lying on the roof. Entire families had been buried in an instant. Further down the road, he met an old lady. He was shocked to see her smiling, and asked her where she was going. She answered simply, 'To church.' Surprised, he said, 'Why are you going to church?' The woman replied, 'I am going to church because I love Jesus, and I want to show others that you can lose everything but have really lost nothing because you still have Jesus.' My father-in-law was completely blown away, and deeply challenged by this woman's words. He later discovered that she had lost her entire family to Hurricane Mitch.

Closing Prayer

Father, the grass withers and the flowers fall, but we thank You that Your Word stands forever. Lord, we praise You that although life is short, we can know You in it. You have not abandoned us; You are faithful through every storm. Help us, Jesus, to dig deep foundations in relationship with You. Amen.

Further Reflection

Lent presents an opportunity for us to lay down some of the things we love in order to pursue Christ and grow in intimacy with Him. Is there something you could stop doing and something you could begin doing to deepen your foundations in Him?

The Humble King

*'Now that I... have washed your feet, you
also should wash one another's feet.'
(John 13:14)*

Icebreaker

In pairs, think of someone you know who is always serving others. Could you come up with a plan to act like their servant over the next week? Consider how you could bless them individually or corporately. Alternatively, you might want to begin the session by washing each other's feet (if people are comfortable with this).

Opening Prayer

Thank You, Lord, that You didn't come into the world to be served, but to serve. Humble King, please help us to think of others more than we think of ourselves. Enable us to be more like You, filled with humility and not pride. We want to be people who serve like You do, seeing and acting on the needs around us. Amen.

Eye Opener

Serving like Jesus is demanding and costly – it requires our all. When my mum had cancer, I remember how weak and pale she looked in the hospital bed. All she wanted was to go and have a wash, but she didn't have the strength to do it herself and the nurses were otherwise engaged. I knew that Jesus wanted me to help my mum in the same way that she had served me for years, so I did. Washing her from head to toe was humbling and amazing. The love between us deepened so powerfully. It meant the world to her.

Setting the Scene

Picture this: the King of the world arrives at a meal with His disciples after a day of ministering in the streets. Their sandalled feet are dusty from their exposure to the elements, having spent hours wandering in the heat and the dirt. Proper etiquette dictates that a slave should wash the feet of guests before the evening meal is served, as foot-washing is considered too humble a task for the majority of servants in the house. But the disciples have still not had their feet washed, and are in no hurry to do it themselves – their priority is to eat and relax!

Yet Jesus does something different. Instead of going with the flow of His followers, He chooses to act in an unusual way. The King takes the role of a servant and gets down and washes their feet. Can you imagine the shock of the disciples? You might be able to detect it a bit in Peter, when he hesitantly says in John 13:6, 'Lord, are you going to wash my feet?' There is a sense of, 'Are you *really* going to do such a thing?!' And the response of Jesus is, 'Yes – you might not know why right now, but you will get to grips with it later.' The Lord is not just going to serve them by washing their feet but by giving up His life on the cross.

Bible Readings

John 13:1–15

'It was just before the Passover Festival. Jesus knew that the hour had come for him to leave this world and go to the Father. Having loved his own who were in the world, he loved them to the end. The evening meal was in progress, and the devil had already prompted Judas, the son of Simon Iscariot, to betray Jesus. Jesus knew that the Father had put all things under his power, and that he had come from God and was returning to God; so he got up from the meal, took off his outer clothing, and wrapped a towel round his waist. After that, he poured water into a basin and began to wash his disciples' feet, drying them with the towel. He came to Simon Peter,

who said to him, "Lord, are you going to wash my feet?" Jesus replied, "You do not realise now what I am doing, but later you will understand." "No," said Peter, "you shall never wash my feet." Jesus answered, "Unless I wash you, you have no part with me." "Then, Lord," Simon Peter replied, "not just my feet but my hands and my head as well!" Jesus answered, "Those who have had a bath need only to wash their feet; their whole body is clean. And you are clean, though not every one of you." For he knew who was going to betray him, and that was why he said not every one was clean. When he had finished washing their feet, he put on his clothes and returned to his place. "Do you understand what I have done for you?" he asked them. "You call me 'Teacher' and 'Lord', and rightly so, for that is what I am. Now that I, your Lord and Teacher, have washed your feet, you also should wash one another's feet. I have set you an example that you should do as I have done for you.'"

2 Chronicles 7:14
'if my people, who are called by my name, will humble themselves and pray and seek my face and turn from their wicked ways, then I will hear from heaven, and I will forgive their sin and will heal their land.'

Session Focus

Humility is such a misunderstood word in our world. We seem to think that being humble means putting ourselves down, not believing in ourselves, or not being willing to put ourselves forward for something we know we'd be good at. Some of us live in fear that we will come across as arrogant or proud if we accept and believe a compliment from another person, or talk confidently about our strengths and talents in an interview.

Interestingly, Jesus is the most incredible example of humility and yet He knew exactly who He was, did what He knew the Father was telling Him to do and did not hold back. The enemy would have us believe that stepping up and doing something well makes us full of pride and self-exaltation, but the truth is this: humility is about *not* thinking of ourselves too highly. It's about knowing that we are no better than anyone else, yet still fulfilling the call that God has placed upon our lives.

We've just read in John 13 how Jesus put aside His evening meal and instead chose to do something selfless. He took up the role of the slave, the lowest of the low – to demonstrate His love. Who is the Christ? Someone who was prepared to get His hands dirty (literally), caring enough to put the disciples' needs before His own, even though it would have been the most uncomfortable and disgusting task – washing animal excrement off hot, sweaty, filthy feet! The challenge for us is, who do we care about more – ourselves, or others?

If I had been at that meal in John 13, I think I could have easily been thinking about how tired and hungry I was, focused only on my belly and which seat I liked the look of the most. I do not think I would have been too concerned about the state of my feet (or anyone else's for that matter!) – it's my own needs that I'd have been looking to meet. And this is western society, isn't it? 'Satisfy yourself first. Take care of number one and then worry about the rest.'

Yet Scripture says that though the evening meal was being served, Jesus got up. We read that 'Jesus *knew* that the hour had come for him to leave this world and go to the Father' (John 13:1, emphasis added). Jesus knew that His time was almost up, and therefore He had to get on with what He knew He had to do. It was time to show the disciples how much He really loved them. Interestingly, this word 'knew' appears in verse 3 and again in verse 11. Jesus knew that the Father had put all things under His power, and He knew who was going to betray Him. He had a far bigger picture of this meal than we do. Jesus was living in the will of His Father, so He knew what He wanted Him to do.

This is challenging: if we knew that we were going to meet the Lord face to face very soon, I wonder how that would affect our behaviour now. I wonder if we would be thinking about those around us more than focusing on our own needs. If you

were one of the disciples approaching that mealtime, would you do something differently?

Jesus was totally focused on His mission – to share His love in humility and service. He was certainly not thinking about what was for dessert, or if anyone was bringing out coffee and after-dinner mints! He didn't care how this extravagant act of service would make Him look, or what people would think. In fact, that was the point – to take on the role of a slave to show His love. He was prepared to get down in the dirt to hint at the extent He would go to make us clean. He is the Humble King. Lord, let us choose to live in Your will, not our own, even if it means being humble like this!

Discussion Starters

1. Do you consider yourself to be humble? In what ways?
   Would Jesus agree that this is humility?

   _____
   _____
   _____
   _____
   _____

2. Do you think that we have misunderstood humility to
   some degree? How do we need to alter our thinking?

   _____
   _____
   _____
   _____
   _____

3. Jesus came into the world to serve, not to *be* served, yet He
   was still a great leader. Do you know any leaders like that?
   What can we learn from their model?

   _____
   _____
   _____
   _____
   _____

4. If you knew that Jesus was returning in a few days, how
   would you shift your priorities?

   _____
   _____
   _____
   _____
   _____

5. Do you sometimes find it difficult to think of others before yourself or are you more inclined to do the opposite? What needs to change? Help each other to answer this sensitively.

_____

_____

_____

_____

_____

6. Are there moments when you know God might be asking you to act differently, but you are worried what others might think?

_____

_____

_____

_____

_____

7. In what circumstances or situations could you display humility like Jesus does in this passage? Have you already found yourself doing it?

_____

_____

_____

_____

_____

8. Spend some time asking God to show you where He wants you to serve Him. If you feel comfortable, share openly with each other.

_____

_____

_____

_____

_____

Final Thoughts

When the Lord begins to speak to Solomon (2 Chron. 7:14) it is after a time of intimate prayer in the temple, where His glory falls. Prayer and humility are closely linked. The more we pray, the more we know the will of the Father and the areas in which He is calling us to humble ourselves. The Lord makes it clear to Solomon that humility is what will lead to breakthrough. If we are going to see Him come and move in our land, we are to seek His face and humble ourselves, turning from our sin and pressing in with prayer. God longs to show us more of His plan, but also needs to work on our hearts.

Having the opportunity to work in Mother Teresa's House of the Poor and Dying challenged me afresh to be the hands and feet of Jesus. Returning to hot showers and proper meals in the UK was amazing but also a reverse culture-shock – I struggled to reconcile what we have with what they don't. But Jesus calls us to keep washing one another's feet wherever we live and whatever we are blessed with. That's the wake-up call we continually need to receive.

Closing Prayer

Humble King, teach us humility under Your mighty hand, and lift us up in times and places where You are calling us to serve. Let our actions be a result of our prayers and knowledge of You speaking, leading and directing our paths. Help us not to be afraid of what others might think, but to be faithful in serving You. Amen.

Further Reflection

Jesus 'got up from the meal' and began to act. Where is the Lord calling you to metaphorically 'get up' from the comfort of where you are and begin to serve Him? Spend some time in His presence, quietly considering if there is an area in your life that needs change.

The Holy King

'Holy, holy, holy is the LORD Almighty;
the whole earth is full of His glory.'
(Isa. 6:3)

Icebreaker

Encourage the group to think of someone whom they consider to be holy. Take time to share these thoughts with one another, going on to share why you think these individuals are holy. Are there overlapping similarities? Are your considerations to do with character, behaviour or both?

Opening Prayer

Lord, You are a holy God. Thank You, heavenly Father, that You reveal Your holiness to us. When You encounter Your children, they stand in awe of You. We praise You, God, for Isaiah and his realisation of Your holiness and how that transformed his life. Lord, we long that we too would want to be holy as You are holy. Amen.

Eye Opener

For the last couple of years, my friend and his family have been ministering in a poor, dangerous spot in Africa where Jesus is changing lives. He told me that as he flew back to England, he observed that it felt 'dark' and different to the country that he had left. The holiness of God was opening His eyes to the darkness of the world. His words challenged me to pray, 'Lord, have mercy on us.' As I prayed, I became increasingly aware of who the Lord is and the need to be 'set apart' as Christians. If the darkness of the world seeps into the Church, we lose the holy presence of the Lord. We live in the world, but we are 'marked out' like Christ.

Setting the Scene

As we turn to Isaiah 6, we encounter a messy world not dissimilar to the one we continue to live in. Isaiah notes that it is the year that King Uzziah died; the sinful, broken king has passed away, leaving behind an even lesser and weaker ruler to take his place. It is fascinating that in the midst of an unstable nation, Isaiah chooses to head to the temple and cry out to God in desperate worship and prayer. He sees a vision of God and His holiness that totally transforms his life.

At the end of these verses we are encouraged, because despite the extremely tough commission Isaiah has to go and prophesy over the people, there is still hope: a holy seed will remain in the land, and though it may be just a stump, not all believers will fall away (Isa. 6:13).

As John pens the words of the Lord to the church in Laodicea in Revelation 3:14–22, he is keen to highlight the importance of holiness. This is the last of the seven churches to be addressed and the words are not comfortable to hear. Those who are lukewarm in faith will be spat out – 'holy' and 'lukewarm' don't go together! The Laodicean church is invited to 'buy' from Jesus gold refined in fire, and white clothes to wear.

Bible Readings

Isaiah 6:1–13
'In the year that King Uzziah died, I saw the Lord, high and exalted, seated on a throne; and the train of his robe filled the temple. Above him were seraphim, each with six wings: with two wings they covered their faces, with two they covered their feet, and with two they were flying. And they were calling to one another:
"Holy, holy, holy is the LORD Almighty;
  the whole earth is full of his glory."
At the sound of their voices the doorposts and thresholds shook and the temple was filled with smoke. "Woe to me!" I cried. "I am ruined! For I am a man of unclean lips, and I live among a people of unclean lips, and my eyes have seen the King, the LORD Almighty." Then one of the seraphim flew to me with a live coal in his hand, which he had taken with tongs from the altar. With it he touched my mouth and said, "See, this has touched your lips; your guilt is taken away and your sin atoned for." Then I heard

the voice of the Lord saying, "Whom shall I send? And who will go for us?" And I said, "Here am I. Send me!" He said, "Go and tell this people: "Be ever hearing, but never understanding; be ever seeing, but never perceiving.' Make the heart of this people calloused; make their ears dull and close their eyes. Otherwise they might see with their eyes, hear with their ears, understand with their hearts, and turn and be healed." Then I said, "For how long, Lord?" And he answered: "Until the cities lie ruined and without inhabitant, until the houses are left deserted and the fields ruined and ravaged, until the LORD has sent everyone far away and the land is utterly forsaken. And though a tenth remains in the land, it will again be laid waste. But as the terebinth and oak leave stumps when they are cut down, so the holy seed will be the stump in the land."'

Revelation 3:14–19
'To the angel of the church in Laodicea write:
These are the words of the Amen, the faithful and true witness, the ruler of God's creation. I know your deeds, that you are neither cold nor hot. I wish you were either one or the other! So, because you are lukewarm – neither hot nor cold – I am about to spit you out of my mouth. You say, "I am rich; I have acquired wealth and do not need a thing." But you do not realise that you are wretched, pitiful, poor, blind and naked. I counsel you to buy from me gold refined in the fire, so you can become rich; and white clothes to wear, so you can cover your shameful nakedness; and salve to put on your eyes, so you can see. Those whom I love I rebuke and discipline. So be earnest and repent.'

Session Focus

Isaiah encounters the Lord in the most incredible way. He can hear angels calling out to one another: 'Holy, holy, holy is the LORD God Almighty.' This is the only time in Hebrew that we see 'holy' repeated a third time – Yahweh is holy beyond anything that language can convey. His holiness is so awesome that the angels have to cover their faces – they just can't handle the glory of the Lord! But what I find most fascinating is what happens to Isaiah: he immediately cries out with intense conviction, declaring that he is 'ruined' and 'unclean'. In the face of God's holiness, Isaiah sees his humanness in a way he has never known before. Not only is Isaiah aware of his own uncleanliness, but his eyes are opened to a land of 'unclean' lips everywhere around him.

When I read this passage again, I wonder whether we have somehow lost a sense of how holy our Lord is? Or perhaps we have never really grasped it? It can feel like we live in a land that says, 'Do whatever you want – God will still love you.' Or perhaps we live with a mindset of, 'How close to the line can I walk and still be acceptable to God? Surely He accepts this as OK? His forgiveness is so great and His love so endless, I am fine.' Yes – it is absolutely true that the love and grace of God reach us in the darkest places, but I also wonder if our Lord is looking for a people who long to be like Him – who want to be holy like Him, and who are choosing to walk towards Him, not away, despite the huge challenges that follow.

Some of the greatest revivals in history seem to have been characterised by a culture of repentance. In 1904, Wales was a nation far from God. However, after years of faithful praying, the Holy Spirit came in power. People flooded into churches, deeply repenting of the sin and mess in their lives. In Hawaii in 1837, thousands responded to the gospel by crying out for mercy, trembling and weeping because of the revelation they'd had of their sin. Like Isaiah, all these new believers had been touched with conviction as the Holy Spirit opened their eyes to the darkness in their lives.

It seems that some nations are currently trying to sweep

away the idea of anything being right or wrong – pushing the philosophy that everything is OK if you are happy with it, as long as you're not hurting anyone. The idea of sin is like a foreign language – as if people are offended by the word itself, and mortified at the very suggestion that it might be something that exists within them. And yet our holy King died for us, sacrificing His life so that we might live. He made a way into the Holy of Holies through what happened at Easter. He longs to make us holy as He is holy.

When I was out running a few months ago, the weather felt so strange that I openly asked the heavens, 'Lord, it's the middle of Autumn – but it is not hot or cold. What is it?!' I believe He responded, 'It is lukewarm, Anne.' I knew that that word was biblical, so when I returned from my run I looked it up in my Bible and was led straight to Revelation 3:16: 'because you are lukewarm – neither hot nor cold – I am about to spit you out of my mouth.' I thought about whether our deeds are making us lukewarm, and whether God is in fact counselling His children again to seek His face. God doesn't give up on His Church. Right here in this passage, He urges us to 'buy from me gold refined in the fire, and white clothes to wear, and salve to put on your eyes to see' (Rev. 3:18). Buy it 'from me', He says – 'don't go to anyone in the world, come to me instead.'

When we encounter the Lord through the power of the Spirit, we are suddenly aware of the awesome holiness of our King. In the presence of the Lord, we can but fall to our knees and repent, knowing that we need saving through the blood of Christ. Perhaps that isn't just a one-time act, but a call to continue being cleansed afresh, and encounter Jesus again.

Discussion Starters

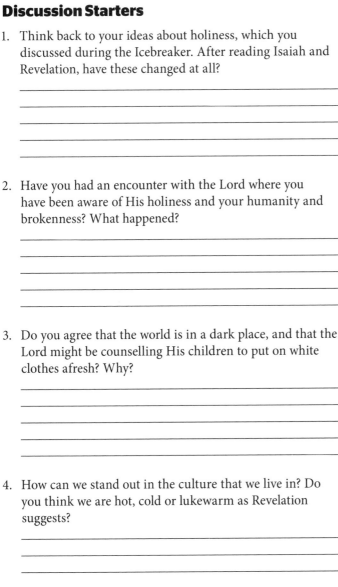

1. Think back to your ideas about holiness, which you discussed during the Icebreaker. After reading Isaiah and Revelation, have these changed at all?

    _____

    _____

    _____

    _____

    _____

2. Have you had an encounter with the Lord where you have been aware of His holiness and your humanity and brokenness? What happened?

    _____

    _____

    _____

    _____

    _____

3. Do you agree that the world is in a dark place, and that the Lord might be counselling His children to put on white clothes afresh? Why?

    _____

    _____

    _____

    _____

    _____

4. How can we stand out in the culture that we live in? Do you think we are hot, cold or lukewarm as Revelation suggests?

    _____

    _____

    _____

    _____

    _____

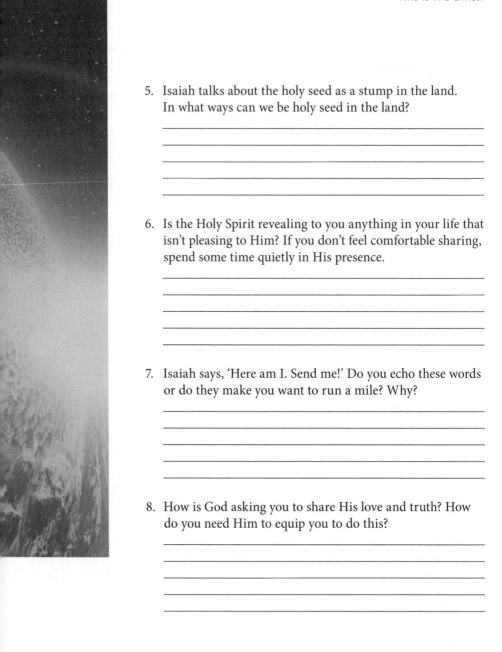

5. Isaiah talks about the holy seed as a stump in the land.
    In what ways can we be holy seed in the land?

    _____
    _____
    _____
    _____
    _____

6. Is the Holy Spirit revealing to you anything in your life that
    isn't pleasing to Him? If you don't feel comfortable sharing,
    spend some time quietly in His presence.

    _____
    _____
    _____
    _____
    _____

7. Isaiah says, 'Here am I. Send me!' Do you echo these words
    or do they make you want to run a mile? Why?

    _____
    _____
    _____
    _____
    _____

8. How is God asking you to share His love and truth? How
    do you need Him to equip you to do this?

    _____
    _____
    _____
    _____
    _____

Final Thoughts

The seraph flew to Isaiah with a live coal from the altar of God, and touched his lips. The Lord effectively cleansed Isaiah in the one area that He wants to use him in – to prophesy over His people. I think God often does that – He cleanses and anoints us in the areas that He will use us the most. Is there an area of your life where it feels like God is doing some 'cleaning out'? Have you had a glimpse of how He might want to use you because of it? Even if the process is a bit uncomfortable, nothing we experience is ever wasted with God.

One of my favourite sayings is this: when we give up, we grow up. That's not to say that a defeatist attitude is a sign of maturity – but rather when we lay things down, we have space to take things up, and when we surrender, we have the opportunity to seek. God isn't calling us to a life of holiness to hurt us. He calls us to holiness because He wants us to know Him more, have greater intimacy with who He is, and share more of His heart with a broken, damaged world. That is what John would call 'life in all its fullness'.

Closing Prayer

Holy King, thank You that You welcome us into Your presence, and You wash us clean by the blood of the lamb. Loving Father, please give us strength to seek Your face and to go Your way. Open our eyes to see what You see, and be willing to go and share You with a lost and damaged world. Amen.

Further Reflection

Spend some time meditating on Psalm 24:3–4: 'Who may ascend the mountain of the LORD? Who may stand in his holy place? The one who has clean hands and a pure heart, who does not trust in an idol or swear by a false god.' As you journey towards Easter this Lent, in the seeking of Jesus' face, allow Him to cleanse and purify you again.

The Harvester

*'Let both grow together until the harvest...
then gather the wheat and bring it
into my barn.' (Matt. 13:30)*

Icebreaker

Sift some flour (or another food item that requires sifting) into a bowl and then look at what remains in the sieve. How does the flour look? What remains in the sieve? Share your observations.

Opening Prayer

Lord, help us to hear what You are saying to the Church in these days. We know that we are called to grow up in the world, and yet be marked out like You for Your kingdom purposes. Father, please cause us to mature like wheat and not become like weeds in our walk with You. Have Your way in us, we pray. Amen.

Eye Opener

Harvesting is fascinating, but unless you're a farmer, the chances are you won't know that much about it! Did you know that weeds and wheat have to grow up together, because the weeds in the field can only be distinguished from the healthy wheat when the seed heads begin to appear? Apparently it is impossible to remove the weeds without damaging the wheat, and so both grow until harvest time. Interestingly, if there is a lack of rain, the weeds can take over and it can stunt the growth of the wheat.

Setting the Scene

Unlike us, Jesus' listeners at the time would have known far more about agricultural practices and were thus familiar with how wheat and weeds grew together, fully understanding His words in Matthew 13:24–30. The kingdom of heaven, and lives lived for Jesus, are like good seed sown in a field. Then an enemy comes and sows weeds among the wheat in an attempt to destroy it. While we live in the world, the enemy will use his weeds to try to destroy the work we are doing for the kingdom. Jesus makes it clear that the weeds and wheat have to grow up together, but this is not for eternity. When Jesus brings in the harvest, the weeds will be completely destroyed but the wheat will be brought into His barn – He will draw His people to Himself, and the work of the enemy will finally end.

Interestingly, Jewish people celebrate Shavuot (the feast of weeks) associated with the grain harvest, which is what the apostles of Jesus were celebrating when the Holy Spirit first came upon them at Pentecost. The Jews commemorate the harvest of the first fruits, but we remember the Holy Spirit coming and the Lord bringing in a great harvest of believers. Pentecost followed the ascension of Jesus into heaven after the events of Easter, and one day Christ will return in the power of His Spirit to bring in a final harvest.

Bible Readings

Matthew 13:24–30

'Jesus told them another parable: "The kingdom of heaven is like a man who sowed good seed in his field. But while everyone was sleeping, his enemy came and sowed weeds among the wheat, and went away. When the wheat sprouted and formed ears, then the weeds also appeared. The owner's servants came to him and said, 'Sir, didn't you sow good seed in your field? Where then did the weeds come from?' 'An enemy did this,' he replied. The servants asked him, 'Do you want us to go and pull them up?' 'No,' he answered, 'because while you are pulling

the weeds, you may uproot the wheat with them. Let both grow together until the harvest. At that time I will tell the harvesters: first collect the weeds and tie them in bundles to be burned; then gather the wheat and bring it into my barn.""'

Acts 2:1-4
'When the day of Pentecost came, they were all together in one place. Suddenly a sound like the blowing of a violent wind came from heaven and filled the whole house where they were sitting. They saw what seemed to be tongues of fire that separated and came to rest on each of them. All of them were filled with the Holy Spirit and began to speak in other tongues as the Spirit enabled them.'

Session Focus

There is so much depth to the words of Jesus! Even in a short parable such as this, there are so many levels to what He is saying. His listeners would have been thinking about their own harvests, fully understanding the agricultural references and well aware of how annoying weeds could be. Perhaps they were also wondering why Jesus was explaining something that they already knew, intrigued as to why he would liken something so ordinary to the kingdom of heaven.

Just so we understand some of the farming process: harvesting was done by hand; the weeds had to be removed first, and then the wheat collected. When there is a decent yield of wheat, the weeds are kept at bay until it is time to gather the wheat.

The weeds of the enemy have the potential to destroy the children of God and choke the goodness out of them, yet we are to grow together in the same field until the day of the harvest. The weeds and the wheat may look the same for a time, but then as they grow it becomes obvious which is which. We need discernment over what is good for us and what is going to damage our growth in Christ. There are things in our lives that may appear to look OK, but God might be saying,

'Don't touch! Watch them turn into weeds.' The weed seed that
is spoken of in the passage is likely to have been from a variety
of rye grass, which is very poisonous. If you ate the seed
it would make you dizzy, with slurred speech, convulsions,
vomiting and diarrhoea. How awful! Yet this is the reality of
messing with what the enemy plants – it makes us ill in body,
soul, mind and spirit. The challenge here is to watch out for
weeds! We are not to separate ourselves from the world – the
'weeds' are left to grow that we might grow stronger too – but
to ask Jesus to give us wisdom from heaven in every area of
our lives, helping us to stay on course with Him.

Also in Matthew 13, we read the parable of the sower
(spoken just before this one). Some of the seeds get choked by
the worries of this world and the deceitfulness of wealth, and
other seed gets stolen away by trouble or persecution. If we are
planted in good soil, we can produce a great crop – it doesn't
mean that we will be separate from the weeds, but that God
will water us as we read His Word, seek His face and serve
Him. Christ is in the business of planting good seeds in our
lives, which He longs to water by the power of His Holy Spirit.
He does not plant anything bad but wants to build up and
nurture what is healthy and strong. The living Lord Jesus longs
to cut off the thorns and anything in our lives that doesn't bear
fruit so that we can grow up healthy and strong in Him. Jesus
lays down His life for us at Easter and then rises from the dead,
overcoming the work of the enemy. Although the weeds still
grow, we have the victory over sin because Christ won it for
us on the cross. As we encounter the Lord and surrender our
lives to Him, we are changed. However, God wants to go on
transforming His children and moving the mess out of their
hearts and lives, so that we reflect His glory to a broken world
and because He loves us so much.

After the resurrection, Jesus ascends into heaven (Acts 1),
but then the Holy Spirit who He has promised to all believers
comes (Acts 2) to continue guiding us into all truth, and
revealing where the weeds are at work in our daily lives. The
fact that wheat needs rain to help it grow serves as a reminder
that we need the water of the Holy Spirit each and every day to

fuel us to grow stronger in Christ. We so often forget to draw on the power of the Spirit, and yet without it we are more likely to be choked by the work of the enemy. The Christ is the only one who can rescue – the only one who can save – and He longs for the faith of His children to increase and to show His power in the midst of our broken, weed-infested world.

I personally long to see a great harvest of believers, so that when the Holy Spirit comes in power and Jesus returns, there will be an unbelievable crop that has seen so much kingdom fruit throughout the generations. Let's pray that into reality!

Discussion Starters

1. Jesus says, 'while everyone was sleeping, his enemy came and sowed weeds among the wheat' (Matt. 13:25). In what ways might we be 'asleep' and unaware of what the enemy is doing?

_____

_____

_____

_____

_____

2. How do you feel about wheat and weeds growing up together? Would you rather separate yourself from the 'weeds'? Why?

_____

_____

_____

_____

_____

3. Until the seed heads appear, the weeds look like wheat. Could there be areas of your life that look OK, but which might not actually be right?

_____

_____

_____

_____

_____

4. A lack of rain means that the weeds can grow faster and overrun the wheat. How can we make sure that we don't run dry?

_____

_____

_____

_____

_____

5. A lack of rain can also stunt the growth of the wheat. Do you feel like your spiritual growth is stunted in any way? Is there anything you can do to change that?

_____

_____

_____

_____

_____

5. Are you aware of other people in your life who might be struggling in their faith, choked by the enemy's work? Pray God's protection over their faith.

_____

_____

_____

_____

_____

7. If you knew that 100 non-believers were about to come to faith in your church, what would you do to prepare for the 'harvest'?

_____

_____

_____

_____

_____

8. One day, Jesus will return to gather the wheat into the barn. Are you ready for that? What do you long for Him to do in your life to get you ready?

_____

_____

_____

_____

_____

Final Thoughts

This parable only talks about the wheat being gathered into the barn, not about what happens to it after that. In order to use the wheat for cooking, it has to be sifted over and over again to get rid of anything that isn't good. As the wheat is sifted, the chaff blows away in the wind and only the strong wheat is left. A really good harvester makes sure that the wheat is sifted well so that it is as pure as possible. Jesus talks about harvesting, knowing that He is the best harvester in the world and throughout history. He sifts us gently and carefully, allowing the rubbish to blow away in the wind of His Spirit at a time and in a place that we can handle. He never pushes us further than we can handle, but equally He never gives up on the grain or leaves it for someone else to sift. Our lives are so important to Him that He gave up His own. Laying down His life at Easter meant that sin was atoned for on the cross and we can live free from condemnation.

Closing Prayer

Father, thank You for the depth of Your Word and all that You long to teach us through it. Please help us to grow up strong in You and not let the weeds of the enemy damage our walk with You. Father, help us to keep being transformed into Your likeness in the power of the Holy Spirit. Amen.

Further Reflection

We live in the light of eternity. As we journey through Lent, let's remember that at Pentecost (the Grain Harvest), the Holy Spirit came and the believers were filled with power, joy and a certainty that God was at work. That Holy Spirit is living in us today. Invite Him to keep equipping and liberating us as we journey towards the ultimate harvest.

The Risen King

'Jesus said to them, "Take off the grave clothes and let him go."' (John 11:44)

Icebreaker

Wrap one member of the group up tightly in a blanket. Be careful not to cover their face! Step back and ask them how it feels to be bound up. Then encourage them to break free. Can they do it? After a few minutes, help them to break free from the blanket.

Opening Prayer

Lord Jesus, we thank You for coming into the world and dying on the cross. Thank You for saving us from our sin, and making a way for us to enter into relationship with You again. We praise You, Jesus, because You defeated death, rose to life and are now seated at the right hand of the Father. Thank You that we can know You and love You. Amen.

Eye Opener

We love *Star Wars* in our family, and eagerly wait for new films to be released. Our favourite films are most definitely the original trilogy – the characters are brilliant, particularly Yoda. He is like the wise sage, directing and helping his Jedi students to use the force and bring good into the universe. His lines, although back to front, are worth repeating. He says: 'The dark side clouds everything. Impossible to see the future is.' The truth is that darkness does affect our perspective, and yet our Lord longs to lead us into His light so that we can see Him and His will clearly.

Setting the Scene

This story has so much to reveal to us about our risen Lord:
His character, His power and His desire to use us in the work
that He longs to do among us. The moment of Lazarus being
raised from death into life and from darkness into light is
truly awesome. Immediately after this passage, the plot to kill
Jesus begins to unravel and yet our Saviour continues to follow
His Father's plan. Jesus will head towards death Himself and
make the same journey to life as Lazarus – only with eternal
consequences for the entire world.

In resurrecting Lazarus, Jesus proves that He truly is the
Son of the living God – because only the Lord of heaven and
earth can give and take away life. He *is* the author of life.
Essentially, Jesus gives Lazarus life at the cost of His own. You
can imagine Him looking into the tomb, knowing that He
would soon be heading for a grave Himself.

Raising a dead man to life would not be a quiet affair! Jesus
does not raise Lazarus from the dead just because of His love
for Him or out of sympathy for Mary and Martha, but in order
to reveal to the world that He really is 'the resurrection and
the life' (John 11:25).

Bible Reading

John 11:25–44

'Jesus said to her, "I am the resurrection and the life. The
one who believes in me will live, even though they die;
and whoever lives by believing in me will never die. Do
you believe this?"

"Yes, Lord," she replied, "I believe that you are the
Messiah, the Son of God, who is to come into the world."

After she had said this, she went back and called her
sister Mary aside. "The Teacher is here," she said, "and
is asking for you." When Mary heard this, she got up
quickly and went to him. Now Jesus had not yet entered
the village, but was still at the place where Martha had
met him. When the Jews who had been with Mary in the

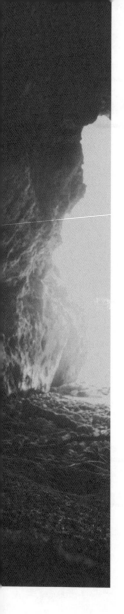

house, comforting her, noticed how quickly she got up and went out, they followed her, supposing she was going to the tomb to mourn there.

When Mary reached the place where Jesus was and saw him, she fell at his feet and said, "Lord, if you had been here, my brother would not have died."

When Jesus saw her weeping, and the Jews who had come along with her also weeping, he was deeply moved in spirit and troubled. "Where have you laid him?" he asked.

"Come and see, Lord," they replied.

Jesus wept.

Then the Jews said, "See how he loved him!" But some of them said, "Could not he who opened the eyes of the blind man have kept this man from dying?"

Jesus, once more deeply moved, came to the tomb. It was a cave with a stone laid across the entrance. "Take away the stone," he said.

"But, Lord," said Martha, the sister of the dead man, "by this time there is a bad odour, for he has been there four days."

Then Jesus said, "Did I not tell you that if you believe, you will see the glory of God?"

So they took away the stone. Then Jesus looked up and said, "Father, I thank you that you have heard me. I knew that you always hear me, but I said this for the benefit of the people standing here, that they may believe that you sent me."

When he had said this, Jesus called in a loud voice, "Lazarus, come out!" The dead man came out, his hands and feet wrapped with strips of linen, and a cloth round his face.

Jesus said to them, "Take off the grave clothes and let him go.'"

Session Focus

This New Testament story is so exciting because it reveals to us that nothing, absolutely *nothing* is impossible with our God! Earlier in the narrative, Jesus had said to the disciples, 'Our friend Lazarus has fallen asleep; but I am going there to wake Him up' (John 11:11). This verse makes me chuckle because Jesus was effectively saying, 'This man is asleep – it's no big deal, I can just go and wake him up.' God's perspective is so entirely different to ours. In the mind of our Lord, death does not signal the end. The reality is that nothing is ever too late for our God. No situation is beyond repair. He can turn *anything* around.

Our God is a God of the humanly impossible, and yet He is also the Lord who feels our pain. We read consecutively in verses 33, 35 and 38 of John 11 that Jesus was 'deeply moved in spirit and troubled', He 'wept', and then was 'once more deeply moved' as He approached the tomb. Seeing the pain of His friends really moved Jesus – He truly is the Lord of compassion. The fact is that no matter what pain we have faced or are going through, Jesus feels it – it hurts Him, and His heart aches with the things that ache in us. Jesus knew what it was like to feel others' pain and His own. Remember Gethsemane? He sweated blood because He knew He had to go to the cross and face excruciating pain.

Yet just as death was not the end for Lazarus, neither is it the end for Jesus or for anyone who turns to Him as their Saviour. In verse 43, Jesus simply said, 'Lazarus, come out!' Let's bear in mind that this man had been dead in the tomb for four days – not four hours, not just a few minutes, but four days! By the time Jesus turned up, the body would have been starting to smell badly. Darkness had the obvious victory. As far as we can see, this man is dead: it's all over for him. And then Jesus goes and calls him back to life with just three words! Some commentators believe that if Jesus had just said 'come out' without specifying Lazarus by name, a whole host of dead bodies would have arisen! It's a completely unbelievable moment: Jesus calls a man to live again, to come out of the

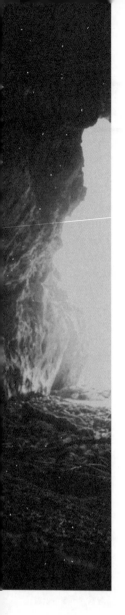

darkness of the grave and into the light of life. This is our God: He is greater than death. He masters it here with Lazarus and He masters it on the cross. He states and then proves that He is the resurrection and the life (John 11:25). Whoever lives and believes in Him will not die but live for eternity with Him. Death loses its sting and the victory belongs to God.

We all have areas of our lives that are in darkness, but Jesus wants to say to each one of us, 'Come out! Walk out of that situation, leave your old life behind and come and walk with me.' He desires to take us into greater life and light, but it requires our letting go of anything that might hold us back. Sometimes life can feel dark, like a cave with the entrance covered by a huge stone boulder, which is impossible to move, but God can bring us up and out of that place. It is not about whether He is able but whether we are willing.

Today's Bible passage ends in such a powerful way: 'The dead man came out, his hands and feet wrapped with strips of linen and a cloth round his face. Jesus said to them, "Take off the grave clothes and let him go."' A mummified man emerges from the tomb shuffling and hopping, with strips of linen covering his face – can you picture it?! The people must have stood there utterly gobsmacked. But notice how Jesus instructs them to move and help Lazarus take off the grave clothes; God asks His children to help one another get completely free. Some of us have walked from death to life but are still wearing our metaphorical grave clothes. Jesus wants to use us to help each other shake off our old life and walk freely with Him.

Discussion Starters

1. In the mind of Christ, Lazarus was only 'sleeping'. Do you sometimes find that you struggle to see difficult situations from God's perspective? Share examples.

_____

_____

_____

_____

_____

2. Nothing is impossible with God. Do you want to challenge this statement or do you feel happy to accept it? Why?

_____

_____

_____

_____

_____

3. If He really is Lord of the impossible, what situation would you like Jesus to turn around? Why not spend a few minutes bringing those longings before His throne in prayer.

_____

_____

_____

_____

_____

4. Jesus felt the pain of Mary and Martha and wept with them. Is there an area of your life where you need to know that He cares? Perhaps you know someone who needs to know that compassion too? Pray for them.

_____

_____

_____

_____

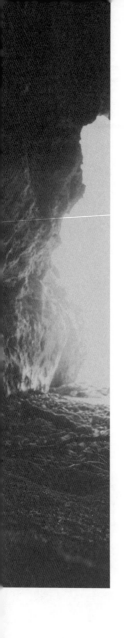

5. Jesus proved that He really is the Son of God. Who do you long to see come into that knowledge that Jesus is Lord?

_____

_____

_____

_____

_____

6. Lazarus walks out of darkness into light. Are there any areas in your life that you want to be liberated from? Perhaps a habit/behaviour you want to stop?

_____

_____

_____

_____

_____

7. Do you have some 'grave clothes' you need to remove and leave behind? How can you help each other do this? Spend some time sharing and praying.

_____

_____

_____

_____

_____

8. Martha says to Jesus, 'if you had been here, my brother would not have died.' Have you ever felt that way towards God? Do you know anyone who currently does? Pray for them.

_____

_____

_____

_____

_____

Final Thoughts

I remember once worshipping at a conference and suddenly
finding myself in tears. I knew the tears were not mine, so I
asked the Lord why I was upset. I felt Him draw my eyes three
rows forward to a lad who sat with his head in his hands. I
sensed that God was weeping over him. After the meeting,
I found a leader who I trusted and we went to speak to this
person together. I told him that the Lord was weeping over
his life and forgave him. At that moment, he fell to pieces and
cried tears like I have never seen before. We sat with him and
then prayed. Afterwards, he shared with us that he had been in
a gang and done some things that he didn't believe God could
forgive. He confessed his sin, thanked God for His forgiveness
and was totally liberated. With the help of the Spirit we
encouraged him to take off invisible clothes that were limiting
him from moving forward with Jesus. It was incredible to
witness! God can reach us no matter what we have done.

Closing Prayer

Father, we praise You that nothing is impossible with You;
that You feel our pain and draw near to us. Lord, thank You
for bringing us out of darkness and into light, and setting us
free from the sin that seeks to entangle us. Help us know that
You are the resurrection and the life, and learn to walk in that
reality daily. Amen.

Further Reflection

Just before Jesus raised Lazarus from the dead, He said,
'Anyone who walks in the day-time will not stumble, for they
see by this world's light. It is when a person walks at night that
they stumble, for they have no light' (John 11:9–10). We know
that God's Word is a lamp unto our path (Psa. 119:105) – that's
a good place to start to help us live in the light.

The Commissioner

'Jesus said, "Feed my lambs."' (John 21:15)

Icebreaker

Go around the group and tell each other what you are thankful for in your life. Then read John 22:14–30 aloud, and share communion together.

Opening Prayer

Lord Jesus, thank You for coming down from heaven to earth, to suffer and die for us. Thank You for defeating death and coming back to life so that we can be reconciled to You, enjoying a personal relationship with the King of kings. Thank You for Your Holy Spirit, who continues to reveal more of who You are to us, and to a lost and broken world through us. Amen.

Eye Opener

When the disciples get to the tomb and see that it is empty (John 20:1–9), we realise that the Lord is risen! He is alive! What I love about Jesus is that He doesn't just go off up to heaven without a word. He makes sure that He speaks to Mary Magdalene to comfort and commission her (John 20:10–18); to Thomas to address his doubt (John 20:27–28); to the disciples to tackle their fear (John 20:19–22) and to Simon Peter to reinstate him (John 21:15–19). Jesus does not jump ship when the going gets tough. He gives us exactly what we need.

Setting the Scene

Let's put ourselves in Peter's sandals for a moment. Just a few days before, he watched His friend and Lord get arrested and tried, and was so consumed with fear that he had denied being one of Jesus' followers three times (John 18:17,25,27). Can you imagine how Peter must have felt after all that? Perhaps, like Judas, he had experienced such bitter agony and shame at his actions that he'd reconsidered his right to live. We can probably safely assume that Peter was at rock-bottom as he witnessed Jesus sentenced to death, crucified, and then buried.

I wonder whether Peter felt abandoned because of his sin. And yet, here in John 21, Jesus comes to Peter. He knows where Peter will be – fishing – and He comes to forgive him, to eat with him and reinstate him as His disciple.

The Lord never gives up loving His children, even when we mess up. His hand of forgiveness reaches us and reinstates us, calling us towards Him and pushing us out to serve Him. Jesus does not abandon us, He just calls us to love Him and feed His sheep. Here is Jesus blessing His children beyond measure as they are overwhelmed by the catch of fish brought into the net by His hand.

Bible Readings

John 21:1–17

'Afterwards Jesus appeared again to his disciples, by the Sea of Galilee. It happened this way: Simon Peter, Thomas (also known as Didymus), Nathanael from Cana in Galilee, the sons of Zebedee, and two other disciples were together. "I'm going out to fish," Simon Peter told them, and they said, "We'll go with you." So they went out and got into the boat, but that night they caught nothing.

Early in the morning, Jesus stood on the shore, but the disciples did not realise that it was Jesus.

He called out to them, "Friends, haven't you any fish?"

"No," they answered.

He said, "Throw your net on the right side of the boat and you will find some." When they did, they were unable to haul the net in because of the large number of fish.

Then the disciple whom Jesus loved said to Peter, "It is the Lord!" As soon as Simon Peter heard him say, "It is the Lord," he wrapped his outer garment around him (for he had taken it off) and jumped into the water. The other disciples followed in the boat, towing the net full of fish, for they were not far from shore, about a hundred metres. When they landed, they saw a fire of burning coals there with fish on it, and some bread.

Jesus said to them, "Bring some of the fish you have

just caught." So Simon Peter climbed back into the boat and dragged the net ashore. It was full of large fish, 153, but even with so many the net was not torn. Jesus said to them, "Come and have breakfast." None of the disciples dared ask him, "Who are you?" They knew it was the Lord. Jesus came, took the bread and gave it to them, and did the same with the fish. This was now the third time Jesus appeared to his disciples after he was raised from the dead.

When they had finished eating, Jesus said to Simon Peter, "Simon son of John, do you love me more than these?"

"Yes, Lord," he said, "you know that I love you."

Jesus said, "Feed my lambs."

Again Jesus said, "Simon son of John, do you love me?"

He answered, "Yes, Lord, you know that I love you."

Jesus said, "Take care of my sheep."

The third time he said to him, "Simon son of John, do you love me?"

Peter was hurt because Jesus asked him the third time, "Do you love me?" He said, "Lord, you know all things; you know that I love you."

Jesus said, "Feed my sheep."'

Matthew 28:18–20
'Then Jesus came to them and said, "All authority in heaven and on earth has been given to me. Therefore go and make disciples of all nations, baptising them in the name of the Father and of the Son and of the Holy Spirit, and teaching them to obey everything I have commanded you. And surely I am with you always, to the very end of the age."'

Session Focus

Some time ago now, I was asking the Lord to give me a word for a group of people that I had the privilege of ministering to at a conference. I was hoping and praying for something exciting and encouraging, so I was a bit shocked by what came to mind. The picture God gave me was of a very overweight person sitting on a chair, and they were consuming, consuming and consuming. Day and night they did not stop eating and drinking – to the point where they could not get up off the chair. They were completely wedged into the chair because they had grown so fat. It was a bit bizarre, and I tried to forget about it, but it would not go away. The more eating and drinking that was happening, the sicker it made me feel. I had decided in the meantime that this was not a word for the conference, but I eventually asked the Lord what it meant. I felt Him say something that shocked me to my core: 'Anne, this is what some of the western Church looks like.'

I am not quite sure how long I spent praying on my knees after hearing those words, but all I could do was repent. Though I didn't want it to be true, I knew in my heart that it was so. After a while I began to seek God as to what we should do, how we could change – was it too late for the Church in the west? Were we in danger of consuming ourselves to death?

My mind was drawn to John 21, after Jesus has risen from the dead and goes down onto the beach to have breakfast with the disciples. This is the moment where He reinstates Peter. I am sure you know it: though Peter had denied Jesus three times before His crucifixion – a betrayal perhaps akin to Judas' – Jesus forgives him. He asks him, 'Simon, do you love me?' And Simon Peter says, 'Yes, Lord, You know that I love You,' and Jesus says, 'Feed my lambs.' Again a second time He asks him if he really loves Him, and again Peter says yes. By the third time you can sense Peter's frustration: 'Yes, Jesus, YOU KNOW I LOVE YOU!' – and again Jesus simply says, 'Feed my sheep.' I felt that the Lord was saying: 'Stop feeding yourselves and start feeding others.'

Later, God highlighted the repeated word 'love' to me in

that same passage; that we don't stop consuming because we have to, but because we want to. If we really, *really* love Jesus more than we love ourselves, then we will do something to feed His sheep. Do I love Jesus enough to want to feed His sheep? This was so deeply challenging to me, and I knew without a doubt that it was a word that was meant to be shared.

Scripture talks about people being 'lovers of themselves' (2 Tim. 3:2) rather than loving God, and this appears to be a chief tactic of the enemy – he convinces us that pleasing ourselves is the way to be truly happy. If we make life about us and what we can get and gain, we forget the most important commandment of all: 'Love the Lord your God with all your heart and with all your soul and with all your strength and with all your mind… Love your neighbour as yourself' (Luke 10:27). True fulfilment in Christ is not about me and my ministry, but Christ and His kingdom.

Our God is a commissioning God. We see that so clearly in Scripture, especially in Matthew 28 where He sends His followers out to make disciples. There are all kinds of things that we spend time consuming, and they are different for all of us. I do not believe the image of the fat person in the chair was just about what we literally consume in terms of food and drink, but how we spend our time and money. I feel deeply challenged about where, when and how I am loving God and His people, ahead of satisfying myself.

Discussion Starters

1. What is the most important thing in your life? Who matters the most to you? Discuss why they are at the top of your list.

   _____

   _____

   _____

   _____

   _____

2. Does God come at the top of your list? Why/why not? How hard do you find it to put Him first? What are your struggles in this area? Share together.

   _____

   _____

   _____

   _____

   _____

3. Why do you think Peter struggled to be honest when asked if he was a follower of Jesus (John 18)? What do you think you would have done if you were him?

   _____

   _____

   _____

   _____

   _____

4. Perhaps Peter wondered if he would ever see Jesus again. Are there areas in your life where you feel that God is absent, or where you cannot forgive yourself?

   _____

   _____

   _____

   _____

5. We all have moments where we know that we have hurt God. Peter jumped out of the boat and ran back towards Jesus. How do you tend to turn back to Him?

_____

_____

_____

_____

_____

6. Do you think that we are in danger of being consumers who think only of ourselves? In what ways do you feel a pull to put yourself first?

_____

_____

_____

_____

_____

7. Jesus the commissioner calls us to feed His sheep – what do you think that looks like? Is it something that challenges you? How could you step out?

_____

_____

_____

_____

_____

8. Our commission is to go into the world and make disciples. Is there anything that the Lord might want you to stop doing so that you are available to serve?

_____

_____

_____

_____

_____

Final Thoughts

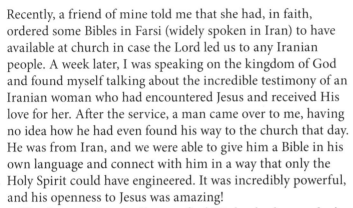

Recently, a friend of mine told me that she had, in faith, ordered some Bibles in Farsi (widely spoken in Iran) to have available at church in case the Lord led us to any Iranian people. A week later, I was speaking on the kingdom of God and found myself talking about the incredible testimony of an Iranian woman who had encountered Jesus and received His love for her. After the service, a man came over to me, having no idea how he had even found his way to the church that day. He was from Iran, and we were able to give him a Bible in his own language and connect with him in a way that only the Holy Spirit could have engineered. It was incredibly powerful, and his openness to Jesus was amazing!

The Commissioner calls us to feed His lambs, but we don't do it alone. We all play our part, led by the Spirit of the living God, and we witness Him change lives. We are commissioned to go and make disciples – not in our own strength, striving to achieve results, but with hearts open to God, asking for His direction while being willing to take risks for the eternal kingdom.

Closing Prayer

Lord Jesus, we need You in our lives. Please help us not to get stuck in consumerism and miss what You are saying and doing in our nation. Father, we need to know Your love and forgiveness so that we can keep stepping out to feed Your sheep. Please show us where, Lord, in Jesus' name. Amen.

Further Reflection

The Commissioner calls us to feed His lambs until He comes back for us. In this season of Lent, as we lay our lives down afresh, surrendering everything to the ultimate lamb on the cross, what can we begin to do to show His love more to a broken world? Why not offer to pray for someone today.

Leader's Notes

General Notes

These studies should be simple to follow and understand. It is worth looking at the Icebreaker section ahead of your time together, in case props are needed. You may want to adapt the prayers with words that flow from your heart, or encourage a time of group prayer. As you read through the Bible verses, the group may feel drawn to another part of Scripture – don't hold back from broadening the picture, as there may be more that God wants to say to you. The illustrations could prompt further stories from other members of the group; please encourage space to share. Remember that the studies serve only as a framework; the goal is to unpack what the Spirit is saying to the Church via every individual.

You may find that the questions can be quite deep and personal for some people, but pray and encourage the group to be as honest as possible by creating a safe space. It may be that some questions generate emotion. Depending on your group dynamics, it might be good to encourage conversation in pairs or threes.

Each study should flow from one to another, the goal being to help each person to grow in their relationship with Jesus. You may find that there is a challenge in the text and it might be appropriate to begin the following session asking what difference or change has come about since the group last met. For example, people may have felt that they were building on sand and not spending time with God – they may make a shift and dig deeper into God's Word or stop doing something that is taking them away from Jesus. Celebrate any ways that the group is drawing closer to Christ.

And have fun!

Study One: The Builder

The aim of this study is to consider 'Who is the Christ?' and reflect on Him as the chief builder in our lives. The desire is that together you can unpack what is governing people's lives and be able to make shifts in how we are choosing to live.

Focus in on the reality that Jesus wants us to hear His words and put them into practice. This is ultimately about spending time not just talking but listening to the Lord. He talks about asking, seeking and knocking – what areas do people struggle with?

The lady in Honduras knew what it was to lose everything yet have lost nothing because she still had Jesus. How dependent are your group on Jesus? Where does their security lie? You may want to pray for each other that Jesus would become more of a central building block in your lives.

What effect are culture and busyness having on this discussion? It may become apparent that people are convicted of having no time to 'build' in Christ. Perhaps you can focus in on discussing together what has worked for people in terms of spending time with God. How have holy habits been cultivated?

If there is time for a testimony, someone may want to share how they were living life without Jesus but then discovered that relationship with Him was more important than anything else.

There may be big hurdles for people in this discussion; things that individuals begin to identify as sand and need to change. It could be as big as making space for people to repent, or make just a small shift in their daily walk with Jesus. Your discernment of this will be partly dependent on how well you know the members of the group. The key is just to give space for sharing and prayer.

Study Two: The Humble King

The aim of this session is to really think about humility – identifying what is real godly humility and what is false humility. How can we begin to really walk in humility like Jesus demonstrated to us through His life (especially washing the disciples' feet)?

The passage from 2 Chronicles is a reminder that if we are really going to see a move of God in the nations then humility is vitally important. Pride and conceit are not going to trigger a move of the Spirit. The emphasis is on the reality that God wants to be God in all our lives; we must not limit, stop or get in the way of Him moving in the situations we find ourselves in.

One of the key points to highlight is that Jesus puts other people first. He gets up from the table, rather than continuing to recline. What situations are we in where we need to get up from where we are and move out? The truth is that this can be very hard in the west, and you may find yourselves discussing why it is so difficult to choose Christ over comfort. Encourage that discussion. The key is intimacy and trust in Jesus. The more we love Him, the more we desire to serve Him.

Make space for prayer. Who wants to walk in humility? Who desires to serve? Who longs to see God move? Ask for the Lord's help.

There may be an incredible servant among you. Honour them and bless them for who they are and the way that they serve in the Church or outside. Encourage others to say what they see in that person too. The greatest servants are often the least recognised, so although this study is on humility, it's worth acknowledging that affirmation and encouragement are important too.

Study Three: The Holy King

The aim of this session is to imagine what it must have looked like for Isaiah to encounter the Lord, with a focus on the truth that our God is so holy and pure that in His presence we realise how broken and messy we really are. The plan is to draw out whether the group has encountered the holiness of God and what difference it has made in their lives.

You may want to focus for a bit on how people are being changed by the Lord. What is He doing in them? Isaiah was cleansed in the area that God wanted to use him in. Are there areas of your life where God is refining you and getting you ready to serve Him in a new way?

As well as considering our own understanding of the Lord's holiness and how He might be refining us, this session is designed to encourage the group to think about the community/nation that they live in. What do they think God sees when He looks at these areas? Are we in a place of darkness or being lukewarm, and why?

A time of prayer for the world, the Church and for us as individuals to encounter the holiness of the Lord again might feel appropriate after this session's discussion.

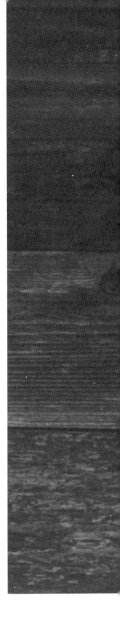

Study Four: The Harvester

The aim of this session is to help the group to focus on Jesus as the harvester, acknowledging that there will be challenges to their faith journey that demand specific prayer and action. Part of this is helping the group to identify that there is an enemy at work sowing weeds among the wheat, and how he might be doing that in their lives and church.

Following last session's discussion over holiness, you may want to ask the group if they feel that the Church is being choked by the weeds of the world, what they are and how we can keep growing strong in Jesus as we prepare for harvest.

There is a caution here not to spread fear among the group – they don't want to leave feeling choked by weeds! However, there is an opportunity to help them identify what is holding them back from going deeper in their faith. This might require vulnerable conversation that could be better done in pairs and followed up with prayer for one another. The goal is to assist one another in finding ways to keep growing up in Christ in a healthy way, disentangling themselves from the weeds so that they will be ready for harvest.

It may be that some people need more 'water' (refreshing by the Holy Spirit) to help them in their growth. There could be others who feel that they are in a 'sifting process' and life is full of challenges right now. Ensure there is space and a trustworthy setting for prayer, and encourage the group that as the harvester, Jesus will return.

Study Five: The Risen King

The aim of this session is to emphasise that God is able to breathe life into anyone, bringing them out of darkness and into the light of knowing Him.

As we think about Easter and a resurrected Messiah, how much are we living in the resurrected life? The curtain was torn in two, enabling us to enter into the holy of holies – intimacy with the King of kings – but are we living in that, and experiencing His power and transformation in our lives?

There may need to be space to share questions that people have for God: areas of struggle and longing. The darkness is so real for people in many different ways. This is a session full of hope but we need a balance, identifying anyone who is waiting for daylight to come. Jesus feels our pain: do we feel one another's pain? As the body of Christ, let's encourage one another towards greater hope and light.

Some of the group may be experiencing areas of darkness in their lives but longing for the grave clothes to come off. It could be appropriate to offer people the chance to seek forgiveness – perhaps taking paper, writing what they want to stop doing/get rid of, folding it up and placing it into a waste paper basket in the middle of the room.

If there is a time for someone to share how they have been freed from a dark place, it could greatly encourage the group.

Study Six: The Commissioner

The aim of this session is to focus the group on the cross, and on Christ's great commission to us all. It is a chance for us to think about who Jesus is, what He has done for us and what He asks of His followers.

This is a moment for the group to consider their priorities again: do they really love Jesus, and know who He is and what He has done for them – or has that reality got a bit lost in the day-to-day of life? The truth is that to be messengers for Jesus, we need to feel deeply passionate about the message that we carry.

Encourage the group to discuss how they feel about sharing the love of Jesus with unbelievers. What are the challenges that they face? Are there methods that have helped others in the group – such as praying for someone or sharing testimony?

How can we actively seek to feed the lost with the truth of Jesus? This comes down to knowing that the Holy Spirit equips us for the task and we are not alone. It is about speaking to those who He is already at work in, and sharing with those who are seeking, with Christ's leading.

Let's not make the great commission an unreachable goal because of our own fear and limitations, or because of what the enemy would like to whisper in our ears. Maybe ask the group to write down a name that they will pray over every day and actively seek to draw to Jesus.

EASTER

WHAT HAPPENS NEXT?

40 Days with Jesus is a post-Easter resource for individuals, small groups and churches. At its heart is an invitation to actively explore the accounts of the risen Jesus and the impact He had on those He encountered.

Written by Dave Smith
ISBN: 978-1-78259-138-2
Bulk order discounts
available for churches and
small groups.

 Also available in eBook formats

01 For you:
A 40-day devotional underpinning the whole series

02 For your small group:
Free video teaching and small group studies

03 For your church:
Free sermon outlines

To find out how you can get involved, visit **40days.info**

Courses and events

Waverley Abbey College

Publishing and media

Conference facilities

Transforming lives

CWR's vision is to enable people to experience personal transformation through applying God's Word to their lives and relationships.

Our Bible-based training and resources help people around the world to:
- Grow in their walk with God
- Understand and apply Scripture to their lives
- Resource themselves and their church
- Develop pastoral care and counselling skills
- Train for leadership
- Strengthen relationships, marriage and family life and much more.

Our insightful writers provide daily Bible reading notes and other resources for all ages, and our experienced course designers and presenters have gained an international reputation for excellence and effectiveness.

CWR's Training and Conference Centre in Surrey, England, provides excellent facilities in an idyllic setting – ideal for both learning and spiritual refreshment.

CWR Applying God's Word
to everyday life and relationships

CWR, Waverley Abbey House,
Waverley Lane, Farnham,
Surrey GU9 8EP, UK

Telephone: **+44 (0)1252 784700**
Email: **info@cwr.org.uk**
Website: **www.cwr.org.uk**

Registered Charity No. 294387
Company Registration No. 1990308